Farleigh Hungerford Castle

Charles Kightly

Introduction

Set in a valley on the border between Somerset and Wiltshire, Farleigh Hungerford Castle was a fortified mansion, occupied for over three centuries by the remarkable Hungerford family. Some time before 1383 Sir Thomas Hungerford (c.1328–97) began building a quadrangular castle with tall corner towers. His son Walter, the first Lord Hungerford (1378–1449), greatly extended the castle by the addition of an outer court and other features during the 15th century.

Thereafter, despite two confiscations by the Crown and many family disasters and scandals, nine more generations of Hungerfords developed the castle as their luxurious home. The chapel is the most impressive of the surviving buildings, with its outstanding medieval, Tudor and 17th-century monuments and wall-paintings. Beneath the chapel is the family vault with its unique collection of human-shaped lead coffins.

During the Civil War, the castle was occupied by the Parliamentarian owner's Royalist half-brother. It was later sold by the notorious spendthrift Sir Edward Hungerford IV (1632–1711) in 1686. By the 1730s it had been partly dismantled for its fittings and building stone. Following further dilapidation over time, partial use as a farmyard, and the adaptation of the chapel into a 'cabinet of curiosities', the castle became a popular romantic ruin. Taken into state guardianship in 1915, it was conserved amid initial controversy, and today remains a striking monument to its distinguished, but sometimes disreputable owners.

The Tour

Built as a quadrangular fortress in the late 14th century, Farleigh Hungerford Castle stood as the impressive residence of the colourful Hungerford family for over three centuries. An outer court which encompassed the chapel was added in the 15th century. The castle developed into a luxurious mansion in the 17th century, before falling into ruin from about 1700.

FOLLOWING THE TOUR

The tour begins near the entrance to the bridge to the inner court, and takes visitors first to the inner and then to the outer court, before moving on to the chapel and finally the priests' house. The numbers beside the headings highlight key points on the tour, and correspond with the small numbered plans in the margins.

◼ INNER COURT

The castle layout incorporates two main areas: the inner court and the outer court. The inner court was the earliest and always the most important part of the castle. It was largely built by Sir Thomas Hungerford between about 1370 and 1383. Housing the chief residential rooms of the castle, it consisted of a quadrangle of buildings inside a square enclosure with a tall round tower at each corner. Protected by a moat on the south and south-west sides, and by steeply falling ground on the others, it was entered via a twin-towered gatehouse. Until about 1700 when the castle began to fall into ruin, visitors would have entered the inner courtyard through the main 'show front' of the castle, with its high walls and impressive towers. These, and all the exterior walls of the castle, were originally covered with white-limed render, rather than left as bare stonework.

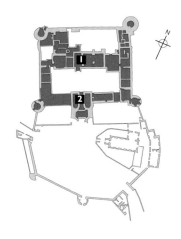

◼ INNER GATEHOUSE

The gatehouse was reached by a stone-paved track (still partly visible) leading to a drawbridge, which crossed the moat at a higher level than the modern bridge. The inner stonework supports of this drawbridge can still be seen. During the first half of the 15th century, Walter Lord Hungerford reinforced the entrance to the drawbridge with a barbican, whose outer face is marked by the arrow-head shaped foundations flanking the modern bridge. The inner gatehouse itself consisted of a pair of round-fronted towers set close together, with a passage about 2m wide between them. Its upper floors probably contained living rooms, and the gateway might have had a portcullis for additional defence.

Below: A reconstruction drawing showing the castle as it might have looked in the late 17th century. A dry ditch faced in stone once extended on either side of the barbican. By this time it had been filled in to create gardens

Facing page: The south-west or 'lady' tower, looking east towards the east gatehouse

Living in the Castle

Wills and inventories help to illustrate the way of life of past owners of sites such as Farleigh Hungerford

The wills of some of the medieval Hungerfords provide glimpses of the vanished splendours of the castle and an insight into the lives of its rich inhabitants. Often bequeathed as heirlooms to be kept for generations, furnishings included expensive imported tapestries for the hall, great chamber and bedchambers. In 1459 Robert, second Lord Hungerford, left new tapestries nearly 60 yards long, depicting hunting, hawking, 'and other divers sports'.

Beds and their hangings were among the most valuable items in a medieval home. At Farleigh, the family's beds had silk, velvet or tapestry-work hangings and silken quilts. Sir Thomas Hungerford's widow, Lady Joan, left a green bed embroidered with a greyhound (a Hungerford family badge) and another with stars and chaplets in her will of 1412. Walter Lord Hungerford left a blue silk bed embroidered with greyhounds, and another patterned with leaves of wood-sorrel in 1449. Other beds had red and blue cloth-of-gold hangings, and one is described as 'a bed of tapestry-work called the "Bed of Beasts", embroidered with cats of the mountain [wild cats]'.

Other wills record sets of rich vestments and altar vessels for the castle chapel, and precious tableware for the hall. The second Lord Hungerford, for example, left over 50 silver and silver-gilt bowls, salts, basins, candlesticks, dishes, flagons and great lidded goblets, as well as sets of silver spoons. Personal treasures included robes lined with ermine, jewelled images of saints, gold and diamond rings, and gold and silver rosaries. However, this was a turbulent period; when he died in 1449, Walter Lord Hungerford left his grandson Lord Moleyns a complete suit of plate armour, 'the best within my armoury at Farleigh Hungerford'.

Above: A jug found during excavations at Farleigh Hungerford
Right: An illustration of the birth of St Edmund from a 15th-century manuscript, showing rich patterned bed-hangings, vessels and other furnishings, similar to ones known to have existed at Farleigh Hungerford

🄳 🄴 🄵 INNER COURTYARD, GREAT HALL AND GREAT CHAMBER

Beyond the inner gateway is the castle's inner courtyard, which is 'pitched' throughout with stones set on edge. A path of large flagstones and bare rock leads from the gatehouse to the central block of buildings – the hall range. Stone steps descend through the remains of the porch to the undercroft beneath the hall, probably used for storage.

The hall itself, which has completely disappeared, was at first-floor level. Local people who remembered it before demolition in the 18th century recalled that it was reached via a porch and a fine flight of about 20 steps. This magnificent room, the principal dining and entertaining room of the medieval castle, was apparently decorated with either carved panelling or wall-paintings depicting men in armour and on horseback. One exaggerated account claimed that it was so large that two broad-wheeled wagons could be turned inside it. At the east end of the hall is the site of the vanished great chamber. Also at first-floor level, this was the principal withdrawing room of the medieval castle. It was reached by a door behind the high table.

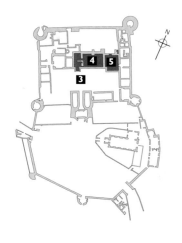

Below: A cutaway reconstruction of the great hall in the 15th century, hung with tapestries

Above: The main drain of the inner court of the castle. Within the drain is a groove for a wooden sluice that could be raised and lowered to regulate the flow of water

THE INNER COURT LOOKING NORTH

1. Great hall (undercroft)
2. Well
3. Kitchen
4. Bakehouse
5. Site of main drain
6. Garden or courtyard
7. Inner courtyard, showing an area of pitching

6 KITCHENS

The service area led off the opposite end of the great hall, to the west. The well with its circular surround stood in an open area. Beyond this, to the left, is the main kitchen, which catered for the Hungerford family, their retinue, and at times for large numbers of guests. In the far wall are the remains of a large fireplace, while set into the wall directly beyond the well is a small rectangular oven. It might have been in one of these fires that the body of the murdered John Cotell was burned on 26 July 1518 (see page 23). Above the kitchen, at first-floor level, was probably a serving area which communicated directly with the great hall.

7 NORTH-WEST TOWER

Beyond the smaller oven and to the right, the circular foundations of the north-west corner tower can be seen below the modern iron railings. Its thick walls surround the original paved basement floor; to the right is the outlet of a latrine pit which drained onto the slope below. Probably known as the Hazelwell Tower after a nearby spring of that name, this tower is said to have housed 'Lady Hungerford's Dining Room', and might have been the prison of Lady Elizabeth Hungerford (see page 24).

8 9 10 NORTH RANGE, GARDEN AND NORTH-EAST TOWER

Adjacent to the north-west tower are the substantial remains of the housing for a brewing copper. Great mansions such as Farleigh Hungerford made all their own bread and ale or beer. Behind the copper-housing is the bakehouse with the remains of its semicircular oven. Outside the bakehouse is one of the

castle's main stone-lined drains, which discharged onto the slope beyond the outer wall. It picked up the waste from a pair of shafts (now covered with a grille) below latrines in a chamber within the thickness of the outer wall. Beyond the drain is a grassed area with a pitched stone path to the right. This was a small courtyard or garden, perhaps a private retreat for the Hungerfords, between the hall block and the outer curtain wall. At the far end of the garden, it is possible to see the foundations of the north-east tower below.

This was the broadest and tallest of the castle's corner towers. It protruded further from the wall than the others, perhaps to protect a vulnerable angle of the defences. An engraving of 1733 shows it standing five storeys high. It was known as the Redcap Tower, either because of the colour of its original conical roof or because a ruin-haunting 'redcap' spirit was believed to lurk there. After undermining by stone robbers, who salvaged stones to re-use in new buildings, this tower fell following a hard frost in February 1797.

11 EAST RANGE

In the corner nearest the north-east tower is a rectangular foundation surrounding a pit covered by a modern grille. This is the latrine tower of the manor house, which existed before the castle was built, and perhaps dates from the 13th century (see page 17). Many later foundations can also be seen along the east range of the castle. During the 16th and 17th centuries this area housed the finest rooms of the castle. By about 1700, the great hall had been largely abandoned as the castle's dining room. Instead, the owners ate more privately in new chambers in the east range, many of which are known to have had large windows filled with heraldic stained glass.

Below: A detail from a sketch of Farleigh Hungerford Castle by Peter le Neve, dated November 1701. His notes describe many rooms now lost, including the old drawing room, the old and new dining rooms, and (doubtless on the top storey) a long gallery and north gallery. The plan also shows the outer bailey and castle surroundings, including a mill

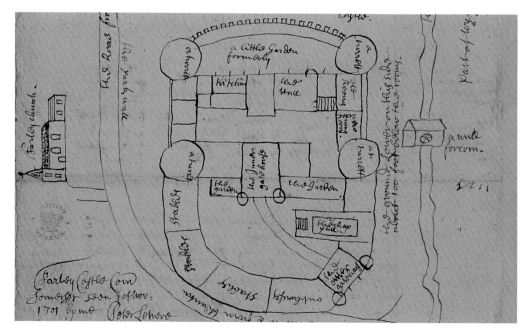

Below: A cutaway reconstruction drawing of the south-west tower (top) can be compared with the remains of the tower today (bottom). It incorporated five floors and was capped by a conical roof

12 SOUTH-EAST TOWER

The south-east tower survives to above third-floor level. What look like battlements on the top are in fact the remains of a ring of windows beneath its original conical roof. High up on the tower to the right can be seen a door, which once led to the wall-walk of the gatehouse front; this indicates the original height of the wall at this point.

Inside, the tower has a circular ground floor with a fireplace, but the upper floors are hexagonal with rectangular windows. Many patches of the plasterwork which would have covered all the castle's interior walls also survive here. The spiral stair which once continued up to the tower roof can be glimpsed in the interior of the wall-walk doorway. A rectangular projection into the moat at the base of the tower contains a grilled-over latrine pit.

13 SOUTH-WEST 'LADY' TOWER

The south front of the castle was lined with buildings flanking the gatehouse. At the far end is the south-west tower. This is the tallest surviving tower, standing five storeys high. A considerable section of it fell on Guy Fawkes Night, 5 November 1842, after children set fire to the network of ivy which held its walls together. Above the ground floor are three floors of circular rooms with fine late 14th-century windows. The top floor is lit by a ring of windows, and the tower originally had a conical roof. To the left are the remains of the stairway within the thickness of the wall, and to the right the base of a latrine pit, which drained directly into the moat.

Also known as the Lady Tower, this was traditionally the site of Lady Elizabeth Hungerford's imprisonment by her husband during the 1530s (see page 24), when local women secretly brought food to her 'great window'. Yet it is hard to imagine how they could have reached any of the windows without detection. It is more probable that her prison was in the north-west tower.

14 WESTERN AND SOUTHERN DEFENCES

Leaving the inner court, turn right to the fragmentary west gateway of the outer court beside the car park. From here, the impressive western defences of the castle can be seen. The dam with a small rubble sluice arch at the centre must have created a pool of water in the ditch against the west side of the inner court. This was supplied with water via pipes from a spring.

A dry ditch, protecting the outer courtyard, continues to the south of the gateway. A walk along this ditch reveals the stub of a small south-west turret and then the outer face of the 15th-century south tower. Its arrowslits are sited so that archers within could shoot at intruders in and beyond the ditch.

15 16 OUTER COURT AND EAST GATEHOUSE

The outer court was added by Walter Lord Hungerford probably between 1430 and 1445. An additional defence for the castle on the more vulnerable south side, it included buildings such as stables and storehouses, as well as the castle chapel. Next to the south tower, the pitched floors of some of the stables, which once lined the whole of this wall, can be seen. The south tower itself, now backed by a wide 19th-century archway, was originally enclosed and entered by a small door.

Dating largely from the 15th century, but perhaps improved in early Tudor times, the east gatehouse was the main entrance to the castle. Above the gateway was a single first-floor chamber, with a door leading to the wall-walk. The slots flanking the window were for the chains, perhaps suspended from wooden beams, used for raising the drawbridge across the outer ditch. From the exterior, the square housing into which the raised drawbridge fitted can be seen surrounding the entrance arch. Within the 'relieving arch' (an arch of masonry designed to strengthen an opening) is a stone carved with the Hungerford sickle badge. Above the window is a worn but splendid carving of the Hungerford arms, flanked at the top right by interlaced sickles, and at the bottom by the initials of Sir Edward Hungerford I (d.1522), who was making other additions to the castle at this time. To the left of the gate are the foundations of a 17th-century house, demolished in about 1805.

17 CHAPEL

Go back into the castle to see the chapel, famous for its monuments and wall-paintings. It was built by Sir Thomas Hungerford between about 1370 and 1383 as the new parish church for Farleigh Hungerford, replacing an earlier one. Sir Thomas's son, Walter Lord Hungerford, enclosed his father's church within the outer court of the castle as part of his improvements to the castle in the second quarter of the

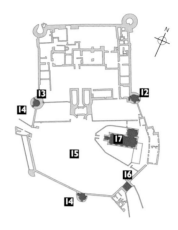

Above: The battlements of the east gatehouse are 19th-century additions. This detail of a watercolour from about 1730 shows that it originally had a four-gabled roof
Below: The outer court looking north. The battlemented wall around the chapel is another early 19th-century addition

15th century. At this time, the church was given new windows and became the castle chapel. Walter built a new parish church on the hill to the south of the castle some time before 1443. The dedication stone from the very first parish church was moved to this building and set above its doorway.

The wall around the chapel dates from about 1800, although the gateway incorporates earlier features, including a carving of the Hungerford badge. Continue round the wall and the north and east sides of the chapel, past the unusual mid-17th-century rectangular windows of the side chapel. Through the gate at the south-east of the chapel is a garden, recently created on the site of the original chapel cemetery. Above the chapel porch is the west window, which is almost identical to the east window of Farleigh Hungerford parish church. The chapel's east window also matches the parish church's west window, confirming Walter Lord Hungerford's work on both buildings in the 1440s.

Chapel interior

At the foot of the steps descending into the chapel is the grave slab, dating from about 1500, of a chantry priest employed to say masses for the souls of the Hungerfords. The skeleton of a young man was found beneath it in the 19th century, described at the time as having 'teeth quite perfect'. The side windows were blocked in the 18th century, and in the 19th century Colonel Houlton, whose family owned the whole Farleigh Hungerford estate, used the space to display his collection of armour. To the right of the altar is the carved and painted tomb of Sir Walter Hungerford IV, 'the knight of Farleigh' (d.1596), and his son Edward (d.1585). The inscription

begins with his motto 'Tyme tryeth truth', and the line against the south wall is designed to be read backwards.

The most notable features of the east end are the wall-paintings. Around the windows are traces of a brocaded foliage pattern. They probably date from the early 1440s, when Walter Lord Hungerford refurbished the chapel. The large figure of St George and the dragon to the right of the window, and a now scarcely traceable figure of a kneeling knight wearing a tabard of the Hungerford arms on the side wall next to it, also date from the 1440s. Both have suffered badly since their discovery in 1844. The red background results from well-meant but disastrous preservative treatment with hot wax, applied between 1931 and 1955 and removed by English Heritage in the 1970s. The paintings originally had a pale background. A later scheme, probably from the early to mid-17th century, includes a magnificent heraldic depiction of the Hungerford arms above the east window.

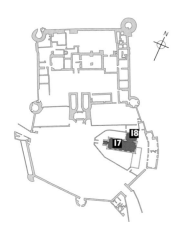

🔢 NORTH CHAPEL

The north (or side) chapel dedicated to St Anne was added in about 1400 to house the tomb of Sir Thomas Hungerford (d.1397), and his second wife Lady Joan Hussey (d.1412).

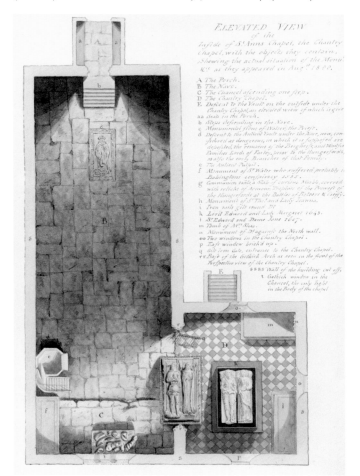

Above: Traces of the 15th-century brocade decoration that can still be seen around the opening of the main east window of the chapel
Left: A plan of the chapel by Thomas Trotter, made in about 1800, showing the layout of the tombs and other features

A Private Paradise

The decoration of the north chapel provides an intriguing insight into the beliefs of Lady Margaret Hungerford and her husband

Above: A portrait of Margaret Hallyday, Lady Hungerford, by Cornelius Johnson, 1631
Below: *A drawing of the chapel in 1842 before restoration, probably by W W Wheatley*

The remains of mid-17th-century wall-paintings are visible in the north chapel. Cherubs with clouds, ribbons and crowns can be seen on the beams, heraldic shields of the Hungerford family decorate the walls, and the figures of two apostles beneath canopies can just be seen in the north-east corner.

Old illustrations show that these traces are only part of an elaborate scheme of painting which once covered the walls and ceiling. Until badly damaged by the partial collapse of the roof in the late 18th century, the ceiling panels were also painted with angels, and more figures of apostles flanked a coat of arms above the north window. The window itself was framed with painted columns disappearing into the distance, and beneath it was a figure emerging from a shroud.

Lady Margaret Hungerford commissioned the paintings between 1658 and 1665 as a backdrop for a tomb she designed for herself and her late husband, Sir Edward Hungerford III. They appear to represent paradise, as described in the Book of Revelation, into which she hoped to awaken on the Day of Judgement. Given the prominent Hungerford heraldry, Lady Margaret perhaps intended it as an exclusive paradise for herself and her family. An extraordinary survival, the scheme is even more unusual for being created by the Puritan Lady Margaret, who, one would expect, would have frowned upon the depiction of saints. Paintings of angels or cherubs are more common, however, and can be seen, for example, on the ceiling of Muchelney parish church, Somerset (c.1665), and also at Bromfield church, Shropshire (c.1672).

Their tomb stands beneath the arch between the main chapel and the side chapel. Sir Thomas is depicted in armour, and traces of the rich paintwork which originally adorned the whole of the tomb can be seen on the lion at his feet. Figures representing the couple's children stand in niches on the north side of the tomb. The wrought-iron railings around the tomb were erected by Walter Lord Hungerford in about 1443.

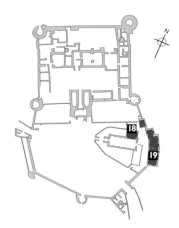

The wrought-iron gates to the left of Sir Thomas's tomb were added by Margaret Hallyday (d.1672), widow of Sir Edward Hungerford III (d.1648), between about 1658 and 1665 as part of her reconstruction of the side chapel to create a shrine for the marble monument in its centre. Perhaps designed by Margaret herself, the monument cost the then immense sum of £1,100. It depicts Sir Edward in his armour as a Civil War commander, with Margaret beside him. She also added new windows to the chapel and the black and white marble paving. This was framed by a scheme of wall and ceiling painting, still partially visible. The north chapel also houses the carved and painted tomb of Sir Edward Hungerford II (d.1607) and his wife Dame Jane, and that of his sister, Mrs Mary Shaa (d.1613).

Burial vault

Beneath the chapel, accessible via an external door on its north side, is a burial vault. It holds the best collection of human-shaped lead coffins in Britain. The coffins still contain the embalmed remains of four men, two women and two children. Four have faces moulded onto them, which may be 'death masks' cast from the faces of the deceased. The coffins probably include those of Sir Edward Hungerford III and Lady Margaret (whose monument stands in the chapel above), and the first wife, son and daughter-in-law of Sir Edward Hungerford IV (known as 'the spendthrift').

Below: The lead coffins in the chapel crypt were originally enclosed in timber, but were badly damaged by 18th- and 19th-century visitors. Some of them allegedly poked sticks through the lead to reach the embalming fluid within, and are said even to have tasted it

19 PRIESTS' HOUSE

Leave the chapel garden and return to the priests' house. This was originally built in 1430 to accommodate the chantry priest employed to pray in the castle chapel for the souls of Sir Thomas Hungerford, his wife and their ancestors. After 1443 it was shared with a second priest commissioned to pray for Walter Lord Hungerford. Following the abolition of chantries during the Reformation, it became a dairy and then a farmhouse, and was extended northwards in the later 17th century. It remained a farm for nearly 300 years, and before 1838 a new granary (now housing the ticket office) was built opposite. In 1959 the priests' house and other farm buildings – the last remaining inhabited part of the castle – were bought by the Ministry of Works and restored to house a display about the castle.

History

Farleigh Hungerford Castle was the home of the Hungerford family for over three centuries. After distinguished beginnings, the family was plagued by misfortunes and scandals during the late medieval and Tudor periods. Divided during the Civil War, the Hungerfords were finally ruined by extravagance in the late 17th century. The castle was then sold and subsequently fell into ruin.

READING THE HISTORY

This section describes the history of Farleigh Hungerford Castle up to the present. It contains a feature on the wall-painting of St George in the castle chapel (page 21) and a family tree (page 32).

THE FIRST CASTLE AT FARLEIGH HUNGERFORD

Farleigh Hungerford Castle stands on a hillside above the Somerset bank of the River Frome, which here forms the boundary with Wiltshire. The name 'Farleigh' comes from the Anglo-Saxon words 'faern-laega', meaning 'the ferny pasture', but this area was first settled long before Saxon times. A Roman villa with a bath house was discovered in 1822 about half a mile to the north.

The land on which the castle now stands was called 'Ferlege' in Domesday Book. From the late 11th century it belonged to the Montfort family, who gave it its earlier name of 'Farleigh Montfort'. They built a manor house here, perhaps in the 13th century, fragments of which are incorporated into the castle. After 1337 the property passed to the Burghersh family, who in 1369 sold it for £733 6/8d (about 430 times the annual wage of a building labourer of that time) to Thomas Hungerford (d.1397). His descendants would be intimately linked with the castle for the next three centuries, and by 1385 Farleigh Montfort was already known as 'Farleigh Hungerford', the name it has borne ever since.

The first documentary evidence for the castle at Farleigh Hungerford dates from 26 November 1383, when a royal pardon records that Thomas Hungerford (by that time 'Sir Thomas') 'fortified the mansion of his manor at Farleigh Montfort with a wall of stone and lime, crenellated, battlemented, turreted and enclosed within a ditch, making thereof a fortress'. Exactly when construction began is unknown, but archaeological evidence from the ruins suggests that it proceeded in stages, with the corner towers, for example, being added to an existing curtain wall. The resulting building was what is now the inner court of the castle, in a version of the latest quadrangular style. It consisted of a rectangle of curtain walls, with tall round towers at each corner, a twin-towered gatehouse, and rooms, including a hall and great chamber, ranged within it.

Sir Thomas was born before 1328. He came from an established Wiltshire family, which had already achieved local influence as members of Parliament and estate administrators, particularly for the Wiltshire lands of the earls of Lancaster. Sir Thomas developed these family interests on a grander scale. By the time he was knighted in 1375, he had become Chief Steward of all the vast southern English and Welsh estates of Edward III's younger son John of Gaunt, duke of Lancaster (1340–99), who by that time was effectively ruling England. Two years later Sir Thomas was elected Speaker of the Commons, the first formally recorded holder of this office, in the Parliament of January 1377. The contemporary chronicler Thomas Walsingham, who disliked Gaunt, was in no doubt about how Sir Thomas got his position: 'Thomas Hungerford was ... a knight on the friendliest terms with the duke, since

Above: A stained-glass portrait of about 1400 of Sir Thomas Hungerford, from Farleigh Hungerford parish church
Below: A detail from the royal pardon of 1383, where the castle of 'Thomas de Hungerford' at Farleigh is mentioned for the first time

Facing page: A 15th-century wall-painting of St George slaying the dragon from the chapel at Farleigh Hungerford

Above: The tomb of Sir Thomas
Hungerford and his wife Lady Joan.
Sir Thomas's head rests on a helm
bearing the crest of a greyhound's
head. Lady Joan's head rests on a
cushion supported by angels, and
her feet on two dogs
Below: The new parish church in
Farleigh Hungerford village. It was
financed by Walter Lord Hungerford
and was completed by 1443

he was his steward: who wished nothing to be pronounced,
other than what would please his master's eyes'. Sir Thomas
held many local government offices. He was sheriff of
Wiltshire 5 times, and Member of Parliament for Wiltshire or
Somerset 16 times. These, and his services to Gaunt, brought
him considerable wealth and lands, including at least nine
manors in western Wiltshire, Somerset and Gloucestershire.

It is curious that Sir Thomas, who was an administrator
rather than a warrior, should want to build a castle at Farleigh
at all. The site offers no outstanding natural defences, and is
overlooked by rising land to the south. He may instead have
been following an aristocratic fashion. Certainly the 1370s and
1380s saw a spate of castle-building throughout England, much
of it also in the modish quadrangular style. Shirburn, Bolton,
Sheriff Hutton, Wressle, Wingfield and Bodiam Castles were
all begun during these decades.

If Sir Thomas's new castle was more of a status symbol
than a serious fortification, his choice of the comparatively
weak site at Farleigh is more explicable. The castle's situation
here may have been due to the fact that there was an existing
manor house suitable for conversion, or to the lack
of rival landowners in the area. Sir Thomas evidently envisaged
the castle as the principal residence for his family and
descendants, as he chose to be buried here in 1397, rather
than at his larger property at Heytesbury in Wiltshire. In 1412
his wife Joan was also buried here in the castle chapel.

THE CASTLE EXTENDED

Between his father's death in 1397 and his own in 1449,
Sir Thomas's son Walter Lord Hungerford (1378–1449)
extended the castle, probably mainly during the period from
1430 to 1445. His additions included the outer court; the
reinforcing barbican outside the gate of his father's original
quadrangular mansion (which now became the castle's inner
court); and a house for the priests employed to say masses
for the souls of his parents in the adjacent chapel, which he
also refurbished.

Walter also raised his family to national importance.
Like his father, he owed his advancement to the House of
Lancaster. When John of Gaunt's son Henry Bolingbroke
became Henry IV in 1399, Walter was knighted on the eve
of the coronation. During Henry IV's reign he undertook
many foreign diplomatic missions, including accompanying
the king's daughter Philippa to her marriage with the king
of Denmark. However, it was as a close associate of the
king's eldest son that he really prospered. When the prince
became King Henry V in 1413, Walter was immediately
appointed to his father's old offices, and became Speaker
of the Commons in 1414.

Already renowned as a jouster, Walter joined the

Agincourt expedition of 1415 with a retinue of 17 men-at-arms and 55 archers. On the night before the battle, according to an eyewitness, it was he (and not, as Shakespeare portrays in *Henry V*, the earl of Westmorland) who wished for 10,000 more archers to reinforce the outnumbered English army, only to be told firmly by the king to trust in God and not in numbers. Appointed Steward of the Royal Household in 1417, Walter then served almost continuously with Henry V in France for five years, overseeing the capture of fortress after fortress during the Hundred Years War. He was well rewarded, and in 1421 received the highest of all military honours, a Knighthood of the Garter. A still greater token of royal trust followed in 1422, when the dying king appointed Walter one of the two guardians of his baby son, the future Henry VI. Walter played a crucial role in the government of England for the next ten years. He was created the first Lord Hungerford in January 1426 and served as Treasurer of England between 1426 and 1432. 'The wise lord baron of Hungerford', as he was known, continued to fight in France, leading larger and larger retinues in attempts to stem the loss of Henry V's conquests. He remained a member of the royal council until his death at Farleigh Hungerford Castle in 1449.

Walter's will reveals that he had become very rich during his long and active life. Through marriage settlements for himself, his children and grandchildren, he added at least

Below: A 15th-century manuscript illustration of the Battle of Agincourt, in which Walter Lord Hungerford fought in command of a large retinue of men

70 manors to the family lands, mainly in the west of England. He also purchased some 40 more estates and properties, including a London town house. After his death he made bequests to dozens of religious houses to finance prayers for the souls of himself and his family, and to the poor of 20 parishes. He also left lavish furnishings for the castle and – a reminder of his family's crucial links with the House of Lancaster – John of Gaunt's own gold and silver drinking cup.

Another source of riches is revealed by the Tudor antiquarian John Leland, who visited Farleigh Hungerford Castle in about 1540. He mentions the 'common saying' that the hall and three chambers 'within the second [inner] court' of the castle were built by one of the Hungerfords 'by the prey [ransom] of the duke of Orleans whom he had taken prisoner'. There is no other record that Walter played a part in the capture of Charles duke of Orleans at Agincourt, but he certainly did take eight prisoners for ransom during the battle, as well as several profitable French captives in later years. These ransoms may well have helped finance his extensions to the castle. But war could also bring losses, and in 1429 Walter was forced to raise the huge ransom of £3,000 for his eldest son, captured by the French. A combination of another ransom demand and continued loyalty to the House of Lancaster brought ruin on the next generation of Hungerfords and the loss of their castle.

Above: An engraving of the seal of Walter, Lord Hungerford
Right: A manuscript illustration showing a city being taken by siege. While fighting for Henry V in 1422, artillery under the command of Walter Lord Hungerford forced the surrender of the French city of Meaux, which had held out for eight months

St George and the Order of the Garter

St George was probably martyred in Palestine in the 3rd or 4th century but it was not until Edward III (reigned 1327–77) declared him the patron of his new Order of the Garter in 1348 that he replaced the Anglo-Saxon St Edmund as England's patron saint. St George's prestige rose still higher under Henry V (reigned 1413–22), who attributed his victory at Agincourt in 1415 to the saint's intervention, and made his feast on 23 April a day of national celebration.

The Order of the Garter was and remains England's highest honour. It is an exclusive group limited to 26 knights including, and chosen by, the sovereign. Most medieval knights of the garter were members of the royal family or distinguished warriors, so the admission of Walter, first Lord Hungerford, to the order on 3 May 1421 was both a mark of high royal favour and a reward for outstanding military service.

The wall-painting of St George in Farleigh Hungerford Castle chapel shows him wearing the style of armour popular in the 1440s, and was almost certainly commissioned by Walter, as part of his chapel refurbishments during that decade. A kneeling figure of a knight wearing the Hungerford arms was originally painted beside it, and probably represented Walter himself.

The romantic legend that St George was a knight who killed a dragon to rescue a maiden was perhaps popularised in England by returning crusaders

Below: A 15th-century enamelled plate that marked Walter Lord Hungerford's stall as a Knight of the Garter in St George's Chapel, Windsor
Left: A manuscript illustration from the 15th century showing Edward III. The badge of the order – a blue garter bearing the motto Honi Soit Qui Mal Y Pense ('shame on him who thinks ill of it') and enclosing the red cross of St George – can be seen on the king's robe

DISASTERS IN THE WARS OF THE ROSES

Walter's son Robert, second Lord Hungerford (1400–59), was in comparison an undistinguished character. His short tenure of the castle was overshadowed by the need to raise another huge ransom for his own son, also named Robert, who was captured by the French at the disastrous English defeat at Castillon in 1453. This ransom eventually amounted to nearly £10,000 – several times the annual income of even the rich Hungerfords. Lord Robert's widow, Lady Margaret, died still in debt in 1478, explaining to her heirs why she could not leave them as much 'as I might and would have done, if fortune had not been so sore against me'.

On his return from six years of captivity in France in 1459, Margaret's son Robert, third Lord Hungerford (usually known by his wife's family title as Lord Moleyns), immediately became involved in the struggle for the English Crown between the Houses of York and Lancaster, known as the Wars of the Roses. Lord Moleyns (c.1423–64), who had a reputation for thuggery, was a close associate of the redoubtable Queen Margaret (1429–82), wife of Henry VI and effectively leader of the Lancastrians. In 1460 he failed to hold the Tower of London against a heavy Yorkist bombardment, and went into exile. In 1461 he returned to take part in the catastrophic Lancastrian defeat at Towton, after which he was attainted (deprived of his titles and lands). Escaping to Scotland, Lord Moleyns continued to maintain the increasingly hopeless Lancastrian cause until he was captured at Hexham and beheaded in May 1464. His eldest son Sir Thomas Hungerford was also attainted, and hanged, drawn and quartered at Salisbury in 1469, allegedly for plotting with Queen Margaret against the life of the Yorkist Edward IV (reigned 1461–83).

The Hungerfords lost Farleigh Castle to the Crown on the attainder of Lord Moleyns, and in 1462 Edward IV granted it to his 16-year-old brother, Richard duke of Gloucester, later Richard III (reigned 1483–5). However, the castle certainly remained habitable, for Margaret (later countess of Salisbury), daughter of Richard and Edward's brother, George duke of Clarence, was born there in 1473. In 1483 the newly crowned Richard III granted the castle to his chief supporter John Howard, duke of Norfolk.

Below: The tomb of Robert, second Lord Hungerford (d.1459), in Salisbury cathedral. He wears the 'Lancastrian' livery collar of SS, and his feet rest on a greyhound, a Hungerford family badge

THE CASTLE RECOVERED

Unlike his father Lord Moleyns and his older brother Sir Thomas, who were both executed, Sir Walter Hungerford II (1441–1516) avoided involvement with the Lancastrians and attached himself instead to the Yorkist Edward IV (as one of the royal household esquires, he helped carry the king's coffin in 1483). However, when Richard III then seized the throne from Edward's sons (subsequently known as the Princes in the Tower), Sir Walter joined the rising against him, becoming leader of the rebels in Wiltshire. Although pardoned when the revolt collapsed, he was apparently detained in the Tower of London.

When Henry Tudor, the heir of Lancaster, invaded in August 1485, Sir Walter was sent under guard to Richard III's army. He escaped, and rode across country to fight with Henry at the Battle of Bosworth on 22 August. Three days later, the victorious Henry Tudor (now King Henry VII, reigned c.1485–1509) knighted him, and early in the following year Sir Walter regained Farleigh Castle. He spent the remainder of his long life in favour with the Tudor kings, and bequeathed the castle to his son Sir Edward Hungerford I in 1516.

TUDOR SCANDALS AT FARLEIGH

Sir Edward Hungerford I followed his father in serving the Crown at home and abroad. He accompanied Henry VIII (reigned 1509–47) to his famous meeting with Francis I of France (known as 'the Field of Cloth of Gold') in 1520. His second wife was a widow named Agnes Cotell, to whom he left all he had when he died in January 1522. Agnes had previously been married to a certain John Cotell, possibly Sir Edward's steward. An inventory of her possessions reveals that they were by no means impoverished, but Agnes clearly felt she could do better. On 26 July 1518 two of her servants, 'by the procurement and abetting of the said Agnes', strangled John at Farleigh Castle with his own linen neckerchief, 'and the body of the said John (was) … put into a certain fire in the furnace of the kitchen in the castle of Farley … and did burn and consume'. Six months later, by now married to Sir Edward, Agnes received the two servants at the castle, 'well knowing that they had done the murder aforesaid'. Though the murder was apparently no secret locally, Agnes and her hired killers remained exempt from prosecution until after Sir Edward's death. But in 1523 all three were hanged for the crime at Tyburn in London.

The castle then passed to Walter Hungerford III (c.1503–40), only son of Sir Edward and his first wife. Walter married three times, but prospered only after his third marriage in 1532 to Elizabeth, daughter of Lord Hussey, who recommended him to Henry VIII's rising minister Thomas Cromwell. Walter became Cromwell's agent in the Farleigh

Above: A 15th-century manuscript illustration of an execution during the Wars of the Roses, in which Robert, third Lord Hungerford, aligned himself with the Lancastrians and was beheaded by the Yorkist King Edward IV

Below: The arms of Sir Edward Hungerford I from above the entrance to the east gatehouse

Above: Farleigh Hungerford Castle from the north-east

area, a service which bore fruit when he was created the first (and last) Lord Hungerford of Heytesbury in June 1536.

By that time, Lord Walter's father-in-law Hussey was out of favour at court, and Lord Walter began to persecute the unfortunate Elizabeth. According to an extraordinary letter she wrote to Cromwell, perhaps in 1539, she was 'continually locked in one of my Lord's towers in his castle … these three or four years past … under the custody of my Lord's chaplain, which has once or twice heretofore poisoned me'. She claimed that she was often reduced to drinking her own urine, and that without the charity of 'poor women of the country' who 'brought me to my great window, in the night, such meat and drink as they had', she would have starved to death. According to tradition, Elizabeth's prison was the south-west tower of the inner court, now known as the Lady Tower. However, she was more probably imprisoned in the north-west tower, which once housed a room known as Lady Hungerford's Dining Room.

We do not know whether Cromwell ordered Elizabeth's release, but on the 28 July 1540 both Cromwell and Lord Walter were beheaded on Tower Hill – Cromwell allegedly for treason and Lord Walter for treason, witchcraft, and the

then capital crime of homosexuality. Contemporaries noted
that Lord Walter had gone mad by the time of his execution,
'for he seemed so unquiet, that many judged him rather
in a frenzy than otherwise'. With him died his title, and the
Hungerfords' ownership of Farleigh Hungerford Castle
reverted to the Crown once more. Elizabeth, 'the lady in the
tower', survived to remarry Sir Robert Throgmorton, with
whom she had five daughters before dying peacefully in 1554.

THE CASTLE IN THE LATER 16TH CENTURY

According to a survey compiled after Lord Walter's execution
in 1540, Farleigh Hungerford Castle was 'very strongly
builded, having inward and outward wards, and in the inward
ward many fair chambers, a fair large hall, on the head [at
the upper end] of which hall are three or four goodly great
chambers, with fair and strong roofs, and divers other fair
lodgings'. It was set in a fine park within a boundary two
and three quarter miles in circumference, containing many
great oaks and other timber trees, and stocked with some
70 deer for hunting. It is not surprising, therefore, that Lord
Walter and Elizabeth's son Sir Walter Hungerford IV
(1532–97) had to pay the considerable sum of £5,000 in
order to buy back the castle from the Crown in 1554. Known
as 'the knight of Farleigh' because of his prowess at field
sports, Sir Walter was famous for his horses, greyhounds and
falcons. He almost certainly updated the castle, adding great
Elizabethan-style windows.

In 1558, after the death of his first wife, Sir Walter married
Anne, sister of Mary I's close friend the beautiful Jane Dormer.
However, ten years later during the reign of the Protestant
Elizabeth I, when Anne's Catholic court connections had
lost influence, he divorced her, accusing her of adultery,
murder and attempting to poison him. These accusations
remained unproved, and Sir Walter was ordered to pay

Above: A detail of the decoration
from the tomb of Sir Walter
Hungerford IV, known as
the knight of Farleigh
Below: An engraving of Farleigh
Hungerford Castle by Samuel and
Nathaniel Buck, made in 1733.
The view appears to show the
hall range between the two eastern
towers of the inner court

THE NORTH VIEW OF FARLEY-CASTLE, IN THE COUNTY OF SOMERSET.

Above: The tomb of Mrs Mary Shaa, sister of Sir Edward Hungerford III. She is shown kneeling at her prayer desk.

Below: A copy of a coat of arms sketched by Peter le Neve in the 18th century, and said to have decorated the withdrawing rooms of the castle's inner court

Anne alimony. He steadfastly refused to do so, preferring instead to remain for some time in prison for debt. Worse still, Anne accused her husband ('that great beast') of wilfully neglecting their Daughters.

The couple's only son, Edward, died young in 1585. His father was later buried with him, beneath a monument still in the castle chapel. By that time Anne was a Catholic exile in Flanders, plotting with the Spanish against Elizabeth I's Protestant government. According to her letters, Sir Walter had attempted to disinherit their daughters, in favour of his illegitimate daughter. Her mother was his mistress, Margery Bright, whom he married shortly before his death some time in 1596. Only then, when Farleigh Castle passed to his brother Sir Edward, did Anne finally get her alimony, enabling her to live in comfort until her death, still in exile, in 1603.

THE CASTLE IN THE CIVIL WAR

The state rooms of Farleigh Hungerford Castle's inner court, already modernised by Sir Walter Hungerford IV, seem to have been improved further in the first half of the 17th century. According to a survey of 1701, Sir Edward Hungerford II (d.1607), added heraldic glass to the 'north gallery' in the east range. His painted tomb can still be seen in the castle chapel, near that of his sister Mrs Mary Shaa (d.1613). Even more additions, including an array of glass in the windows of the 'old drawing room', 'old dining room' and 'gallery', were made by Sir Edward's great-nephew and heir Sir Edward Hungerford III (1596–1648). This Sir Edward is also buried in the chapel, beneath a magnificent monument depicting him in full armour as an English Civil War general. His widow Margaret, shown beside him, commissioned the monument and the redecoration of the side chapel between about 1658 and 1665.

Despite the military appearance of his tomb effigy, Sir Edward Hungerford III played an undistinguished part in the Civil War of 1642–47. A Puritan and Member of Parliament, his marriage to Margaret Hallyday, daughter of a Lord Mayor of London and stepdaughter of the earl of Warwick (later Admiral of Parliament's navy) brought him into the inner circle of those who opposed Charles I's policies.

When the quarrel between the king and Parliament flared into civil war in 1642, Sir Edward therefore thought himself the obvious candidate to command Parliament's forces in Wiltshire. His local rival Sir Edward Baynton thought otherwise, and each man imprisoned the other in turn before Parliament decided for Hungerford in January 1643. Sir Edward Hungerford however, rarely paid his troops, and was rumoured to embezzle wages due to them. He abandoned in turn Salisbury, Malmesbury (twice) and Devizes to the Royalists, although he did take Wardour Castle in Dorset by siege in May 1643. He fought at the drawn battle of Lansdown, but escaped from the Parliamentarian rout at Roundway Down, thanks only to the speed of his horse. Neither did he succeed in holding Farleigh Hungerford Castle, which at this time witnessed the only known military actions in its history.

At the beginning of the war, the castle was held for Parliament by Sir Edward Hungerford, although there is no record of a garrison there. But after the king's capture of Bath and Bristol it was taken over (apparently without fighting) by Royalist troops under Sir Edward's own half-brother, Colonel John Hungerford. This Cavalier garrison was reportedly 'very troublesome' to the surrounding country, commandeering supplies and horses, and in September 1644, a surprise Parliamentarian cavalry raid succeeded in carrying off 60 horses from beneath the very walls of the castle. A second Parliamentarian force then arrived, but 'declined making any attempt' to attack. Later in the same year the castle was recorded as being used as a storehouse for 'suits of apparell' for the Royalist armies.

In March 1645, a Royalist force was attacked at nearby Trowbridge by the Parliamentarian Sir William Waller, and was forced to take refuge within the castle. However, when Parliament's all-conquering New Model Army took first Bath and then Bristol, the outlying garrison at Farleigh stood no chance of survival. It surrendered (again apparently without fighting) on 15 September 1645. Colonel John and his officers were permitted to ride away with their weapons, while his soldiers walked off disarmed. Sir Edward resumed control of the castle, but he refused to install a garrison there, and the castle saw no further action. It seems to have suffered little or no damage during the fighting.

Above: A damaged iron pikeman's pot helmet of the Civil War period, said to have come from the castle armoury

Below: The tomb of Sir Edward Hungerford III (d.1648) and his wife Lady Margaret Hallyday, in the castle chapel. Erected between 1658 and 1665 and perhaps designed by Lady Margaret, the monument cost the large sum of £1,100. Sir Edward, in full armour, holds his commander's baton. His feet rest on the corn-sheaf and sickle badge of the Hungerfords, and his wife's on the lion and anchor crest of the Hallyday family

FORVM
VTILITATI publicæ per quam necefsarium
·REGIA CAROLI 2ⁿᵈannuente MAJESTATÆ.
proprijs Sumptibus erexit perfecitq
D.EDOARDVS HVNGERFORD
Balnei Miles
ANNO MDCLXXXII

*Above: A 19th-century engraving
of the bust of Sir Edward the
spendthrift, which once adorned
a building overlooking Hungerford
Market in London. The building has
now been demolished*

*Below: A watercolour, thought to
date from about 1730, showing the
castle from the south-east. It clearly
shows the conical roofs that
originally topped the corner towers,
the west service range with its high
chimneys. and the main castle gate*

Sir Edward died 'most peacefully', but childless, at Farleigh Hungerford in 1648, so the castle passed to his half-brother Anthony Hungerford, who had been a rather half-hearted Royalist during the Civil War. Despite fines levied on him by Parliament, Anthony died a rich man in 1657. His son, the last of the Hungerfords to own the castle at Farleigh, would become notorious as Sir Edward 'the spendthrift'.

FARLEIGH AND SIR EDWARD THE SPENDTHRIFT

Sir Edward Hungerford IV (1632–1711) made a lavish financial gift to Charles II (reigned 1660–1685) just before his restoration to the throne in 1660. It was reported by a contemporary that 'not three men of the nation … made the like present'. According to tradition, he sumptuously entertained Charles and his court at Farleigh in about 1673. However, despite this early extravagant support for the king, he was opposed to Charles II's plans for his Catholic brother James, afterwards James II (reigned 1685–1701) to succeed to the throne. In 1680, indeed, he was among those who attempted to have James brought to trial. As a result he lost his local offices, and when the Rye House Plot to assassinate both Charles and James came to light in 1683, Farleigh Hungerford Castle was searched in vain for weapons. Thereafter Sir Edward frequently sat in Parliament, but never spoke. Possibly he remained a member only because it exempted him from arrest for debt.

Sir Edward's debts and extravagances were legendary. He is said to have spent 500 guineas on a fashionable periwig, and gambled away a manor on a single throw at a bowling match. Absorbed with the need to raise money, he was in 1670 among the founders of the Hudson's Bay Company, which sought to exploit the resources of Canada. Less

successfully, he promoted weekly markets on the site of the dilapidated Hungerford mansion in London: 'Hungerford Market' much later became Charing Cross station. Yet in 1686 he had to sell nearly all his West Country estates, including Farleigh Hungerford Castle, to Henry Baynton (the grandson of his Parliamentarian uncle's rival, Sir Edward Baynton), for the immense sum of £56,000. Even this did not clear his debts, and he died a pensioner 'poor knight of Windsor' in 1711.

The sale ended three centuries of Hungerford ownership of Farleigh Castle, and though Henry Baynton and his wife Anne (daughter of the still more notorious Restoration rake, the poet Lord Rochester), lived there for a few years, the castle's days as a habitable residence were almost over.

DESTRUCTION AND DECAY

The castle was sold for salvage in 1705 to the Houlton family, and over the next 30 years was systematically reduced to ruin for its materials and fittings. Among these were its elaborate 17th-century fireplaces. The dining-room chimneypiece alone fetched £40 – twenty times the annual wage of a scullery maid at that time. Marble floors were taken up (some went to pave the gardens of Longleat), panelling was sold, and in the 1730s many of the inner court's buildings were taken down to provide stone for Joseph Houlton's new 'Farleigh House' on the far side of the village. So well-constructed were the ancient walls that 25 labourers worked for nearly a year to demolish them. After Mr Houlton had taken his pick, local people were allowed to remove whatever they liked, and ornamental fragments of the castle long

Above: This engraving from about 1774 shows the extent of the dilapidation of the chapel shortly before it was repaired in 1779. The ruins of the now-lost north-east tower can also be seen in the background

Below: An early photograph of a 17th-century chimneypiece at Farleigh House – Joseph Houlton's new country house built on the other side of the village in the 1730s. This might have been taken from the castle when its fittings were salvaged for the new building

adorned village cottages. Long afterwards elderly villagers remembered the splendours of the great hall, with its noble flight of steps and walls decorated with knights in armour.

Thereafter, the decline of the castle continued inexorably. All four towers, though ruinous, are shown still standing in an engraving of 1733, along with some of the inner courtyard buildings. By 1797 the north-west tower had disappeared, and in that year the tall north-east tower, weakened by stone-robbing, collapsed. The outer court, used as a farmyard, suffered less severely. The priests' house, converted into a farmhouse and extended northwards in the late 17th century, long continued in use. At the time of the 1851 census it was occupied by William Greenhill, a dairy farmer who employed six labourers, with his wife and seven children. The family were still running the farm at the turn of the 20th century.

After a long period of dereliction, the chapel was re-roofed in 1779 by a distant Hungerford relation. By 1832 the owner, Colonel John Houlton, had turned it into 'a sort of repository of curiosities', decked with armour, fanciful furnishings, and what were dubiously alleged to be Oliver Cromwell's own jackboots.

RESTORATION AND CONTROVERSY

Many of these changes were recorded in guidebooks compiled by the Revd J E Jackson, curate of Farleigh Hungerford from 1832–45 and a great friend of the castle until his death in 1891. Under his guidance, the inner

Right: A photograph of the interior of the chapel from the 1907 sale catalogue, when the whole estate was sold to Lord Cairns. The chapel was still being used to display a large collection of armour, most of which is now at the Royal Armouries